VIRTUAL MEETINGS WITH POWER AND PRESENCE

The Ultimate Guide to Online Meetings

Praise for

VIRTUAL MEETINGS WITH POWER AND PRESENCE
The Ultimate Guide to Online Meetings

"Although it was acceptable to 'wing it' the first few months of the pandemic, it's time to raise the bar! 'Virtual Meetings with Power and Presence,' does more than provide guidance on the electronic setup and framing for the best experience for your audience. More importantly, this book includes valuable information about dynamic body language, expressing an 'engaged presence,' and yes...even appearance! Now you can differentiate yourself as you move past 'good enough' and get back to being the executive and leader you were pre-pandemic!"

Brian Roberts, Executive Coach and Peer Group Facilitator, Vistage Worldwide

"Virtual Meetings with Power and Presence is a valuable resource that covers all the elements of having a credible online interaction with clients!"

Addie Moray, VP, Production Management, Smithsonian Channel

"Everybody does Zoom calls for work or with family and friends, but the vast majority of us have no clue about doing it the right way. Kim Foley not only tells you WHAT to do and HOW to do it but explains WHY in a really clear and easy-to-understand way."

Joe Yasheroff, 12-time Emmy Award-Winning Producer

"Kim Foley helps perfect your online image and interactions with practical, easy-to-implement techniques. I know, because she's been a trusted advisor to me. Her book is a must-read for anyone who wants to navigate today's video-driven world with confidence and success."

Alaina Love, CEO, Purpose Linked Consulting

"For years Kim Foley has helped me get ready for my television appearances. Now with this book, she is sharing her experience to help you look great in virtual meetings. Get it and learn!"

John Feinstein, Author

"Confidence is very compelling. Kim Foley explains how to present yourself in the most credible and engaging way by sharing her techniques and experience in 'Virtual Meetings with Power and Presence. Kim Foley is known for preparing people for their big moments. Now, with this book, you can benefit and be ready for your big moments."

Kate Gross, Director, TM Center, Bethesda, MD

Virtual Meetings With Power and Presence

The Ultimate Guide To Online Meetings

First Edition

ISBN - 13: 978-0-615-47576-9
ISBN - 10: 0615475760

Professional
Business
Strategies Publishing

8301 Loring Dr.
Bethesda, MD 20817

Author: Kim Foley
Editor: Janet Hulstrand
Designer: Lissa Levinson

Acknowledgments

With so many people struggling to adjust to the sudden onslaught of frequent online meetings, I felt compelled to document what my clients were telling me: working from home has its advantages, but there are also real struggles and challenges to deal with.

As a speaker, I am confident and full of positive energy. But as a writer, I sometimes struggle to find just the right words, and tone. I knew this book would only happen if my friend Janet Hulstrand, who is a brilliant editor, would agree to help me with it. She edited my first book, *The Credibility Factor;* and now she has wrangled my sometimes vague thoughts and ideas into a clear, coherent guide for anyone who is communicating virtually. Her suggestions and changes have been much appreciated, and her creativity, encouragement, and editorial skill have helped this project soar.

Thanks to Lissa Levinson for making this book graphically reflect the excitement I feel about the subject matter through color and design. A true artist!

Special thanks also to Clare Foley, for her sharp eye for proofreading, and for her insightful suggestions.

Thank you to my friend and mentor, Joe Yasheroff, who brainstormed with me as this book took shape. And, to Herb Perone for all his input and suggestions.

Thanks to my husband, Matt, who taught me all the intricate details of how to maximize internet connection, and for cheering me on and listening patiently as I shared what I learned in all my research for this book.

To my children Matthew and Katie: Thank you for your support and inspiration.

And to my beloved cat, who kept me company and was always willing to share a snuggle in the midst of all that social isolation.

This book is dedicated to all of the first responders who are helping us get through a very difficult time with commitment, grace, and courage.

Kim Foley

Introduction

Many people are struggling with online meetings. And for good reason!

Video conferencing feels threatening to most people. They may not like the way they look on camera. They may not know how to use the technology, or they may have no idea how to light themselves, set up a pleasing background, frame themselves on the computer screen — or even figure out where their eyes should be looking.

Sound familiar?

On top of that, deep down most people are terrified of public speaking, and now, with so many business meetings being held via Zoom or other virtual platforms, they are frequently being thrown into a scenario where they're pretty sure they're going to look bad or make a fool of themselves for all to see.

For more than 30 years, as a video producer, media trainer, and television stylist, I have helped high-profile individuals enhance their credibility.

What is credibility? Credibility is simply the ability to be believed, respected, and trusted. Enhancing your credibility is the goal of this book. My purpose in writing it is to help people take control of how they are perceived on a video screen, whether that screen is on a phone, computer, tablet, or camera in a television studio; and whether it is a live interaction or a prerecorded video.

In this book the word video refers to any live platform (such as Zoom, Skype, Webex, etc.) or prerecorded video on any device for online meetings, presentations, social media videos, email marketing videos and other similar activities.

If you have a product, service, idea, or piece of information that you want to share, online meetings are a great way to share your information. And whether you are making your presentation in person or via a video screen, all the research shows that optics matter.

But video is somewhat more challenging. During an important in-person meeting or presentation, you would not slouch, appear disheveled, or be still munching on your breakfast. The stakes of video interactions (online meetings) are the same as in-person meetings; but because most people do not know how to improve the visuals, or how to bring their personal best to this format, they are sabotaging their credibility and undermining their credentials and reputation. Many people may feel that online interactions make them feel a bit removed from the interaction because of using a video screen. This has led many people to think that how they look and interact doesn't matter. To put it bluntly, they are wrong!

In my consultations with executives, managers, and those in leadership positions, I have learned that companies are often thrown into online meetings and presentations unexpectedly, with no time to think about how their teams are being perceived.

All the research shows that in terms of messaging, the next-best thing to being in-person is connecting with video. But to make video that is worth watching, some forethought and preparation are required.

If we have a choice between looking at a well-lit, well-framed, and compelling presentation versus one that makes you look like you have been chained to a desk in a dark basement, which one do you think will compel your viewers to be inspired and engaged, or to buy into and trust what you are saying?

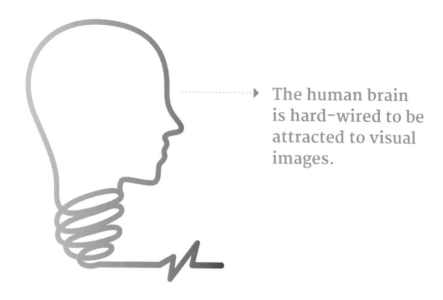

The human brain is hard-wired to be attracted to visual images.

Why is this? Well it is primarily because our brains love to take in the subliminal information provided by facial expressions, body language, voice intonation, visual appearance, and so much more. When we are interacting with another human being, whether we are with them in person or via a video screen, within seconds we are taking in hundreds of visual and audio cues; then, not consciously, and unfairly, we are making assumptions about them.

For most people these assumptions are not meant to be judgmental, but they do create a quick internal narrative that can help us determine if we feel safe with another person, and whether we can trust or believe them. **Hundreds of subliminal cues shape our assumptions of others about a host of things: their intelligence, competence, health, socioeconomic status, credibility, and many additional factors.**

So, in your online interactions, your credibility is at stake, just as it is during in-person interactions. The visuals that others see will either enhance or undermine your credentials.

This book is dedicated to helping you get it right!

CHAPTER ONE

Optimize Your Internet Connection, Computer, Tablet or Phone for Online Meetings

O nline meetings can be challenging for many people because of technical difficulties. So first of all, let's explore all of the ways you can get the best internet connection and speed to support streaming platforms such as Zoom, Webex, Skype, and others.

If you have had difficulty with a good connection in the past, the information below is going to help you immediately improve the quality of what you see and hear in your meetings. However, remember, this is a two-way street. You can send out a beautiful, strong signal, but if the person you are connecting with has a poor connection due to the scenarios below, they may not be able to send one to you.

Anyone can run a free internet speed test to see their megabites per second. Go to www.speedcheck.org to check your download and upload speed. Anything around 30 MBPS or more is good.

Online video streaming platforms need a strong signal in order to be able to support audio and video. If your router is hardwired into your device, then you will have a much better result than if you are using WiFi. If you are using a WiFi connection, how far away your device (computer) is from the router will affect your speed, and therefore the quality of your audio and video in your meeting.

If you cannot get closer to your router, there are excellent products such as Eero, Google Mesh, and Orbi that can boost the strength of the WiFi in your location.

An important factor affecting the quality is how many other devices on your network are streaming online meetings or YouTube, Netflix, homework platforms, etc., at the same time while you are online. This will impede your internet connection. Keep in mind, you are sharing a finite amount of bandwidth with others in your house; this will have an effect on the quality of your audio and video when streaming.

It is really important to take several steps any time you are having a poor signal. These steps will usually boost your speed. **The first one is to reboot your router by unplugging the power cord from the back** (either from the wall or from the device); wait 10 seconds and plug it back in. This will usually help increase your speed. It will take about 5 minutes for it to fire back up.

The next step is to reboot your computer or device. Also, always make sure that all of the applications that you will not need for your meeting are closed before you log onto your conferencing platform. With these steps, you will have optimized your device for the best possible internet speed, and therefore better quality video and audio in your meetings.

You can do everything you've learned in this book correctly, but if you don't know how to maximize your internet connection, you will have undermined your best intentions!

If you have an upcoming meeting that was scheduled by someone else, make sure that you are clear about which platform your meeting will be hosted on. (Don't assume everyone uses the same platform as you.) Then download the platform to your device before the meeting.

Do not wait until 10 minutes before your meeting to explore a new video conferencing platform. In advance of your meeting, get familiar with the settings and make sure that your microphone, if you are using one, is recognized by the platform.

Now that you know all the ways to have a stronger connection, you can jump into the following chapters and learn how to frame, light, get better audio, and much more.

Say goodbye to looking mediocre onscreen; we are going for spectacular!

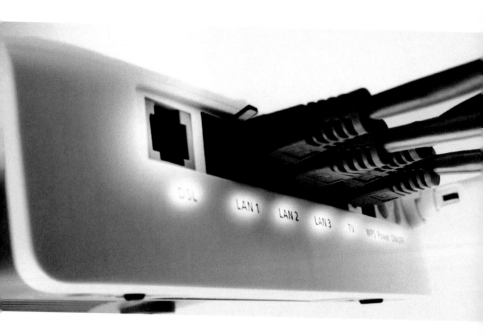

Framing and Angles

W e've all seen people sitting at their desks with their ceiling in the background. Or with the camera pointed at the furniture in their room, or a window, instead of directly at them. These are classic rookie mistakes!

In preparing for a meeting, you need to leave at least 10 minutes to set up the shot and get your lighting, angles, and framing just right.

Some people use the embedded cameras from their desktop computers or laptops, while others use tablets or webcams for online meetings. No matter what you are using to create video, you must make sure that the camera is at your eye level. I don't mean "kind of" at eye level, but **actually** eye level. This is very important, and it's important whether you are sitting or standing.

I repeat: the camera lens always needs to be at eye level. Always! If it isn't, you risk having your viewers staring at your chin instead of your face; or getting dizzy from watching your ceiling fan spin around; or becoming distracted by whatever else is going on in the background.

By getting the angle and framing right, people can see you in a way that mimics you sitting across the table from them. This is the goal, because it makes it easier for them to look at your face, connect, and engage.

You can get the camera at the right level by placing your laptop on boxes, books, or whatever you can find that is flat and level. If you are using a tablet or phone, use a tripod. You may want to get an adjustable platform on which to place your laptop computer just for this purpose. Remember the goal: get the computer or other device's camera lens to your eye level.

I sometimes like to stand for my online consultations, and I didn't want to buy a standing desk, so I bought a lightweight end table that I can place on top of my worktable. It is 19 inches high, and when I place my laptop on it, the camera is 5'3" from the floor — perfect for my height.

There are many ways to accomplish the goal of getting your computer camera at eye level. It all comes down to figuring out how you intend to use your space, and how much you want to spend.

If you are using a tablet or smartphone, instead of a computer, consider getting a mini tripod, which works well for tabletops if you are standing. Some tripods come with holders for your device. If you plan on standing sometimes, be sure to get a tripod that goes high enough to raise your device to eye level when you are standing up straight.

This is how you should be framed, chest up shot, with minimal headroom.

Once you get the camera at eye level, do a test shot to fine-tune how you are framed. This is where getting the right angle comes in. Simply tilt your laptop screen, or device, forward. Remember, first get your camera at eye level, and then adjust the tilt to get rid of the ceiling and headroom. You want your image to fill the frame.

Your on-camera framing should always look like this:

In most situations, the middle of your chest should be at the bottom of the frame. This called a chest-up shot.

This is a chest up shot with too much headroom. The quick fix: pull the video screen forward to reduce headroom.

Let's get specific: a chest-up shot starts about four inches or so below your armpit. Do not frame yourself closer than that to the camera! Closer shots make viewers feel like you are invading their personal space.

The top of your head should be barely below the top of the frame. If you are doing a presentation where you are going to be the focus instead of slides, you might want to consider standing; in that case, you would set up the camera so it frames you from the waist up (you still need the camera to be eye level). It is not necessary to stand while presenting, but many people prefer it because it allows them to widen out to a waist-up shot, and use more body language — for example, to move their hands, in order to create a more dynamic presentation.

If you're speaking or presenting, stand up and back up so people can see more of your body.

However, if your hands are going to be seen by the viewer they should be seen the whole time that you are on camera, and not just pop up into the frame now and then. You can achieve this with a waist-up shot. And don't forget: even if you're standing, you do not want to leave a lot of headroom — just remember to tilt the screen forward before you begin, to get rid of any extraneous headroom.

Even when you are framed tighter (from the upper chest), you can use your hands to add energy to your presentation; but be sure to keep them low (around your waist) so they don't distract your audience by flying up into the middle of the frame.

If you intend to hold something up in the frame — for example, a product you are discussing — always frame yourself from the waist up. You don't want the object you are showing to block your face.

This all sounds more complicated than it is, and you'll get so much better with just a little bit of practice. The most important thing is to remember to leave plenty of time to prepare so that you won't be flustered when the meeting or presentation begins.

Here is a photo of one of my clients: first before, and then after our consultation. In the before photo the window was behind him. I asked him to place his desk in front of the window to get beautiful light on his face.

Before: Lighting behind him   *After: Lighting in front of him*

Once you've experimented with lighting and framing a few times, practice it — maybe even write down what works best in your space, so you can set it up that way every time.

CHAPTER THREE

Optimal Lighting

One of the most critical aspects of looking trustworthy and professional in video meetings is your lighting — and it is also one of the least understood and most overlooked elements.

There are two main issues that need to be addressed to get the lighting right for your online meetings:

- The light in the background (what is behind you)
- The light in the foreground (how the light falls on you).

Remember that the camera on your computer, phone, or tablet does not capture detail in poorly lit conditions, because the processors are not as large and robust as those in a professional camera.

The bottom line is that to deliver a sharp image that is pleasant to look at, these cameras need a lot of light. If you or your background appear dark, it can make you look foreboding or downright creepy.

The main rule to remember is that the background should never have more light than the foreground.

Here is an example of what happens when you forget this rule. (The term for this effect is that the image is "backlit." You do not want that!)

When you have the right lighting, you look vibrant and healthy. Your face may look shinier than it does when you glance in the mirror, because the light that you need to shine on your face in order to produce a well-lit image may reflect off the natural oils on your skin. This is why I recommend using a translucent or blotting powder for any online meeting, for both men and women. We will discuss this more in Chapter 8.

There are many ways to go about getting beautifully balanced light to fall on your face. Daylight is always the most flattering kind of light. The ambient light that a window will provide is ideal unless you are online after dark.

When using natural daylight is not possible, there are dozens of lighting options at many price points that you can buy to address your lighting issues. However, before you decide to buy special equipment, look around your house and see if you already have lights in the house that can be used for

Place your desk or table in front of the window so that you are facing the window. This will work well as long as you are not getting direct sunlight on your face.

this purpose. For example, you may have a pole lamp that can be moved into your space to reflect light off of the ceiling to create indirect, ambient light. Or you could use a small desk lamp like the one to the right made by Room Essentials for $7. This is an easy and inexpensive way to get direct light onto your face.

Sometimes a table lamp, moved behind your computer screen, will provide just the right amount of light for your face. Try it, both with the shade off and with the shade on, to see what works best. Keep in mind that the goal is to get the light either **behind** your computer screen, or to the sides of the screen, so that it shines on your face.

If you have recessed lights, try turning them on and seeing how that looks. Recessed lighting can help light the general area as long as it is not right over your head, which will create shadows under your eyes and chin.

Usually you will need to augment overhead lights with a task light at eye level behind your computer, shining toward your face.

If you have no choice but to set your computer where there is a window in the background, close the blinds and curtains, or get a shade for the window. If you do not have blinds, shades, or curtains, you can tape some heavy white paper over the windows. You will need to do something in order to counteract the backlighting.

People often ask me if warm or cool lighting is best. I prefer to have warm lighting in my home for a softer ambiance, but on-camera you will look fresher, and better, with cool light. Sometimes when you purchase lightbulbs, they are described as daylight-balanced light. These, or LEDS, are the best choice; however, don't let this get in the way of trying to use what you have.

Remember, it will probably take trying several different options to find the perfect set-up for your home: be willing to experiment, and be patient. The results will be well worth it. Keep receipts so you can return what's not working, until you find the best lighting for your particular set-up.

CHAPTER FOUR

Creating the Best Sound

Your internet connection will definitely affect what you see and hear on your screen. Online interactions have two issues when it comes to audio:

- **Other people hearing what you have to say (depends on the quality of your microphone)**
- **What you are hearing (depends on the quality of your speaker or headphones)**

The quality of the sound you are projecting, as well as the sound you are receiving is affected by your internet connection. The other factor that will affect how others hear **you** is whether you are using an external microphone (highly recommended), or the built-in (embedded) microphone on your computer or tablet.

When you are listening to others, what you hear will be affected by whether you are using headphones or a headset (highly recommended), or the embedded speaker on your computer or tablet.

You can review the instructions for improving your internet connection and speed in Chapter 1.

If you hear an echo when you are speaking, it means that you are using two audio sources (such as a phone and a computer); to correct this, turn one of the sources off.

Here is another helpful tip that you can use only if you are working in a quiet space with no ambient background noise, such as traffic, lawn mowers, or people talking. Go to the audio settings on the platform you are using; if there is an option to turn off the "optimize or enhance sound" feature, make sure it is **unchecked**. This setting is there to help mitigate ambient noise, but it will also reduce your sound quality; if your space is totally quiet you don't need it.

If possible, try to find a space that has lots of soft surfaces (like upholstered furniture and carpeting), which will help to absorb sound. This is going to work much better for audio than a room with all hard surfaces, which will reflect sound.

Being heard well by others is the goal. The built-in microphone of the computer is not close enough to your mouth to provide good audio, and it tends to pick up any other ambient noise in your environment. This is where an external microphone can make a big difference.

But there are so many options for external microphones — so how do you know what kind of microphone is right for you?

There are many factors to consider when picking the right audio solution for you. When I am consulting with clients to find their best solution, I have to take the following questions into consideration:

- **Will they be primarily attending meetings? Or primarily hosting or presenting?**
- **Do they need a wireless mic (because they will be standing, or presenting)?**
- **How many hours a day are they typically talking to others online?**
- **What type of device are they using?**
- **Are they using the computer's microphone, or a webcam?**

There are pros and cons to every audio solution, and this decision depends on the answers to the above questions. What you don't want to do is use the microphone attached to your wired earbuds. This is fine for family and friends, but it is not appropriate for business meetings or interacting with clients.

Microphone Options

Computer, phone or tablet microphone: Not recommended, because the internal microphone is not close enough to your mouth to create adequate sound for professional meetings or videos.

Wired earbuds: Not recommended for business.

Bluetooth earbuds: Better than nothing, but they do not have the quality needed for business meetings.

Wired lavalier: Inexpensive (under $25); works very well for business meetings, presentations, or on-camera video. Highly recommended.

Bluetooth lavalier: Expensive; works very well for business meetings, presentations, or on-camera video. Highly recommended if you are a speaker online or you are producing videos.

Wired microphone on a stand: Not a great option because it gets in the way, and is visible to the viewer.

Wireless Bluetooth headset with two earphones and a microphone: Too large, heavy, and not necessary for video business meetings, presentations, or on-camera video.

Wireless headset with one earphone and microphone: Less noticeable, lightweight, and creates the ability to hear well and be heard well. Highly recommended.

I use a Bluetooth headset that has one headphone, and a microphone when doing consultations online. It's lightweight, so I can wear it all day. The only downside is that I have to remember to charge it every night. I also have an inexpensive ($25) wired lavalier microphone that plugs in via USB to my computer, to use when my headset is not charged. Both of these options work very well.

CHAPTER FIVE

Backgrounds: An Intimate View Into Your Life

M ake no mistake: now that so many people are working from home, we all find it fascinating to peek into other people's workspaces and see what is in their backgrounds.

Your background is a visual representation of how you live in your space. And like it or not, people will make assumptions about you on the basis of what they see in the background of your virtual meetings. What they see on their screens adds an important piece of information to the overall story you are telling about yourself.

Your background can either enhance or detract from the overall appearance you are projecting. Your professionalism is on display; therefore, it's important to take a look at what other people are seeing when they look at your image, and ask yourself if your background is contributing to the impression you want to make.

Ideally, you will have chosen the quietest room available to you, with a neutral and uncluttered background.

Let's break it down.

You have three choices when it comes to setting up your background:

- Tidy up the background, and light it appropriately.
- Hide the background with a pop-up screen (I recommend a white one).
- Use a virtual background with a green screen (but get professional advice about how to do it correctly).

Lighting the Background

Many people have been thrown fairly rapidly into the world of online meetings and aren't aware of certain fundamental lighting techniques: for example, it's not only important what people can see in the background, but also how it is being lit.

There's a fairly simple solution for this: you need to bring in a light source. You may need to bring in lighting from other areas of your home, or purchase a light source that can brighten the area, or set up in such a way that you are facing a window. What is going to work best for your space? It could be a pole lamp, a task or desk light, a utility light, or for a large space, an LED panel light.

Choosing the right lighting is one of the main issues that I help people tackle in my one-on-one consultations. Ideally you should light the background without causing shadows. Are there any lamps in your home that can be repurposed? If not, there is an abundance of specialized video lighting you can buy online that may be the solution for you. (See Chapter 4 for more detail about lighting options.)

Composing the Background

Start by asking yourself these questions:

- What do others see in my background?
- Are there items that appear to be growing out of my head (for example, a lamp, a sculpture, or a plant)?
- Is the background cluttered and disorganized?
- Is there anything causing a reflection?
- What items should be removed from the background or tidied up? Are there piles of paper all over the place? Has your child left some of his toys in your work area?
- Are other people walking around in the background?

You may be able to simply shift or turn your computer slightly to change what is showing in the background. If that's not possible, you may have to either change what's in the background, or change the location from which you do your online meetings.

Working from home may mean a limited set of choices as to where you can set up. I once had a meeting with an executive who had set up his computer with the kitchen in the background. Needless to say, there was something of a mismatch between his leadership role and the background he had chosen for his call. I suggested that he purchase a white pop-up backdrop that could be folded up easily at the end of the day.

Virtual Backgrounds

Some people choose to use virtual backdrops, for a variety of reasons. They may be trying to look more professional, but they may actually end up making things worse. For example, if you do not know the techniques of tweaking the level of exposure, you may end up with your hair or ears disappearing from the screen. This is called "keying out."

Virtual backgrounds work best if you use a green screen behind you. This makes it easier for the application to remove the background, separate you from the background, and keep the edges from blurring together. A green-screen background can be created in a variety of ways: with a piece of fabric; a pop-up screen that is on a taut wire, which can fold up easily; or a pull-up green screen. These options have very different price points.

The most important things to understand when using a green screen are that it has to be taut (no wrinkles), and it has to be evenly lit (no shadows).

Not all computer processors are able to support a virtual background. If not done properly, virtual backgrounds can also sometimes be distracting, and are not always appropriate for a business call. Choose a simple white or gradient gray to keep all the attention on you. It's great to have fun with virtual backgrounds during calls with your friends and family — but if you want to use it for business calls or meetings, you should get advice from a professional to make sure that you are using it appropriately and getting good results.

The other reason people are trying out virtual backgrounds is for privacy. I totally understand wanting to keep your personal space private. Sometimes, people are forced to have meetings in very challenging spaces! If this is your situation, you may want to consider using a physical pop-up video or photography screen instead of a virtual background.

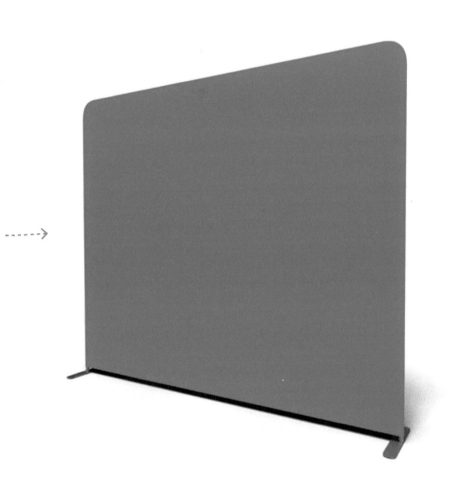

CHAPTER SIX

Should You Use a Webcam?

H aving a clear visual image of your face is paramount in order to foster online engagement in virtual meetings. If your embedded camera makes you look blurry, it could be one of these five issues, or a combination of several of them:

1. The lens could be dirty. If it is a camera in a tablet or laptop it is most likely getting handled quite a bit, and may be covered with layers of oil from your fingertips. Get a soft cloth and clean that lens! This can make a huge difference.

2. It could be an older camera that just doesn't have the technology needed for a sharp image when streaming. If so, maybe it is time for you to upgrade, or get a webcam.

3. The camera could be malfunctioning.

4. You may have a poor internet connection.

5. It may be due to poor lighting.

If you are a speaker, or you are going to be hosting multiple webinars, you may want to consider getting a stand-alone webcam, which offers a big step up in video quality for online streaming.

What is a webcam?

A webcam is any camera that can send video over the internet, whether it is embedded into your computer or attached to your computer via cable.

High-quality video presentations need more than just great content delivered well. The quality of the image, with the right framing, appropriate angles, good sound quality, and a suitable background all work together to make your presentation more than just good — it can be spectacular!

The quality of built-in computer video cameras varies greatly. In order to have a sharp image, you really need an HD-quality auto-focus camera. That being said, you do not want 4K resolution because it uses way too much bandwidth. HD cameras also facilitate easy adjustments for essential settings such as brightness, color, frame rate, and resolution.

Remember, without adequate lighting, the video camera that is in your computer will not have its best image.

Embedded cameras need a lot of light to process detail. So before you consider upgrading to a better camera, first test out some lighting options to see if your image improves. You can review the details about lighting in Chapter 4.

Before you purchase a stand-alone webcam, make sure that the computer you will be using has ports that can handle its cabling. The computer must also be able to meet your webcam's software processing needs.

There are many HD cameras that are available for purchase online, with reviews that highlight the pros and cons of each webcam.

Some of the things you want to look for are:

- Auto-focus capabilities
- USB plug
- Resolution of 1080p (Most platforms cannot support 4K)
- Compatibility with your PC or Mac.

Good-quality, name-brand webcams will cost $79 to $300. Some webcams come with a microphone, but I would still use a dedicated microphone to get the microphone closer to your mouth, creating better sound. The webcam microphone will most likely be better than the quality of sound you can get through your computer, but it won't be as good as what you could get with a dedicated (external) microphone.

Keep in mind, if you have a poor internet connection, using a webcam and microphone will help, but your image and sound will still be less than ideal.

If you have not upgraded your internet speed in a long time, or you have an older computer (more than five years old), you may not have the processing ability to have good quality images when streaming virtual meeting platforms. Less expensive computers have poor quality cameras, which can lead to a fuzzy or blurry image.

If you have done the steps outlined in Chapter 1 to improve your speed and it does not do the trick (which it will 90 percent of the time), contact your service provider to see if resetting on their end resolves the issues.

CHAPTER SEVEN

Dynamic Body Language

I n-person meetings have the advantage of showing the whole person. Unfortunately, because people are often self-conscious in online meetings to begin with, and because they are usually pinned to a chair during the meeting, they tend to not use their hands or facial gestures at all — and if they do, they may convey things that they really didn't intend to convey.

Our body language helps us to decipher communication, inspire others, and express ourselves with more precision. But reading body language cues doesn't only involve recognizing socially relevant visual information: it involves interpreting them as well.

It's important to understand and utilize the power of body language in order to present yourself in a way that is dynamic and interesting anytime that you are on the screen.

When you are hosting a meeting or giving a presentation, your body language can help you engage with your viewers as well as making you appear more powerful and memorable to others.

According to researchers Dr. Marwa Mamoud and Professor Peter Robinson of University of Cambridge, "Body language is a powerful form of non-verbal communication providing important cues about the intentions, emotions, and motivations of others. When hand gestures are performed with emotion regions of the brain are adding meaning to the affective cue interpreted."

By taking the time to understand this much-studied communication skill, you can gradually integrate the suggestions below into your habits, and reap the benefit of becoming a more relaxed and confident communicator whenever you are in front of a video camera.

What is body language?

Body language is the sum total of all of your nonverbal communication; it refers to your facial expressions, eye contact, posture, hand gestures, stance, and all of your body movements.

Do you know what you are broadcasting with your body language?

Why is understanding this so important?

Understanding body language is essential because people often unintentionally sabotage themselves with poor body language, both in person and on screen. If you are not aware of what you are saying nonverbally, you may be sending out contradictory information; you may be verbally saying one thing, but your body language may be saying something else. This is confusing for the people you are trying to communicate with.

Using Your Body Language to Express an Engaged Presence

Certain actions can summon up some unintended assumptions about you. If you are scrolling through your phone, playing with a pet, leaning back in your chair, staring into space, or getting up and moving around, you will probably give others the impression that you are not paying attention to what is going on in the meeting. If you must do something else while participating in a video meeting — for example, answer the door or get a child to be quietly engaged somewhere off-screen — as a courtesy to others in the meeting, turn off your video until you have resolved the issue.

When it's your turn to speak, encourage others to engage with you by looking (at least most of the time) directly at your camera lens, not at the

other people on the screen. This is the best way to make the other viewers feel that you are talking to them.

Don't be tempted to look at your own image. Looking at yourself means you are not looking into the viewers' eyes. It may also prompt you to play with or fix your hair, or engage in other grooming actions. Avoid doing any preening while in a meeting! That should be done before the meeting starts, during the preview of the meeting.

During the meeting, sit up straight — leaning toward the camera can cause odd distortions of your face and neck, and sitting back makes you look tired and worn out. Shoulders should be directly over your hips. If you have a long day of meetings, try placing a small pillow behind you to give your back a little extra support. And unless you are taking notes, try to avoid looking down.

Don't be reluctant to nod or give other positive feedback, such as making a thumbs-up sign when appropriate. A pleasant look on your face coupled with good eye contact into the lens of the camera will really help let others know that you are engaged and interested in what's being said.

Some people find it helpful to tape a photo or piece of colored paper right behind the lens to make it easier to remember that you should always be looking at the lens, not at the screen.

Place colored paper behind your camera lens to encourage eye contact with your viewer.

Whether you are sitting or standing, always keep your body squarely aligned in the frame: this posture tells others that you are engaged and interested.

The question I hear most when it comes to on-camera presentation skills is, "What should I do with my hands?"

If you are sitting, you can and should still use your hands. However, you should keep them low (about waist-high), so they will not pop up randomly into the frame, which is very distracting to viewers. Hand gestures actually help with communication whether people can see them or not; moving our hands is a natural way of expressing ourselves. Using your hands when you speak automatically gives you more energy and naturally causes you to bring more inflection to your voice, so you don't risk sounding monotone.

If your hands are going to be seen on the screen, your palms should be open and held relatively close to the body, because the camera tends to focus on whatever is in closest proximity. Also, your hand size may be distorted if your hands are too close to the camera.

Head tilt

Some people have a tendency to lift their chin when speaking on camera. This can be interpreted as an arrogant gesture and should be avoided; also, it draws more attention to your neck than your face. Keep your chin level when listening or speaking. You don't want the camera to focus on either your hands or your neck: the focus should always be on your face.

Body Language to Avoid

Touching your hair: This often-unconscious cue may lead others to see you as nervous.

Stroking your face: This is a cue that the listener is either self-soothing, or may be skeptical about what they are hearing.

Pointing at the viewer or at your video screen: This may be seen as threatening or aggressive.

Crossing your arms: Though this may only mean that you are cold, others may perceive this as a sign that you are angry, defiant, or that you disagree with what is being said.

Using hand gestures that are higher than your shoulders: Be careful with this gesture — it may work for an entertainer, but it tends to look overly exaggerated on a video or computer screen for business interactions.

Gestures that are too big: Avoid gestures that go off of the viewing screen; they look sloppy, and can be distracting to the viewer.

Using gestures stimulates the speaker's brain, as well as the listeners, during verbal communication. According to The Science of People, when researchers analyzed hundreds of TED talks, they found that the least popular speakers used an average of 272 hand gestures during the 18-minute talk. The most popular TED talkers averaged 465 hand gestures! For more detailed information on how to use your body to engage your viewers, and support your message, pick up *Captivate: The Science of Succeeding with People* by Vanessa Van Edwards.

Remember, smiling is a sign of trust and friendliness. Viewers are naturally drawn to a relaxed and warm persona, which a genuine smile can communicate.

CHAPTER EIGHT

The Power of Image: Clothing, Accessories, Makeup and Glasses

T he notions surrounding the word credibility have tremendous psychological and emotional power, but the word is seldom, if ever, mentioned to most of us while we are growing up. Ask five people what credibility means, and you'll probably get five different answers.

Credibility equals trust. The concept of credibility permeates our subconscious.

We are constantly trying to understand the people around us by absorbing concrete information, as well as subliminal cues given out by the images they project and their body language.

One of the main reasons we observe visual cues is to establish credibility: Can I trust this person? Is what they are saying true? Do they know what they are talking about?

Think about it: when we see someone in an online meeting, on a video, or on TV, their credentials are not always apparent. So we quickly sum up the person's demeanor, image, tone, and body language to determine their credibility.

As a television stylist, media trainer, and video producer, credibility is always foremost in my mind as I prepare my clients, visually and verbally, for live or online presentations and appearances. This is because just as we all do when we meet someone in person, those seeing you in online meetings are in a constant process of making judgments based on what they are seeing and hearing. They are making important assumptions concerning the level of education, social status, wealth, temperament, health, and moral and ethical values of the people they see.

Therefore, your image, which includes the overall effect of your hair, clothing, makeup, speech, voice tone, and body language, is one of the most powerful tools you have. It can be used to maximize your potential. Unfortunately, it can also undermine you.

I'm the first to acknowledge that in a perfect world, we would all be judged on our honesty, our best skills, and our real values — but the sad truth is that often before we have a chance to demonstrate or share any of those things with others, we are judged, and sometimes dismissed, simply on the basis of the image we present. Study after study has shown this to be true. This is not fair, but it is real.

The assumptions others make about our intentions, motivations, tastes, and values can keep us from getting the jobs we deserve, the relationships we desire, and the opportunities that we yearn for.

So why do so many people sabotage their own efforts? Maybe your image just hasn't been something you've thought much about. You are confident about your work and the skills you have to offer your organization, so you just get up in the morning and put on whatever clothing strikes you as comfortable or convenient at the moment, or the only clothes you have that are clean. But if you feel that you're going to impress people with just your track record and what you have to say, not the way you are dressed or the way you present yourself, you may end up being unfairly underestimated.

Consciously or unconsciously, you have chosen the image that you now have — but you should know that you can also choose to change your image at any time. Simply ask yourself this question: "What image is going to get me the best results for this particular situation?"

Too many people make the mistake of wearing what they **wish** was appropriate instead of what really is appropriate. Your closest friends and family will look past your appearance and see your strengths and weaknesses, no matter how you present yourself. But the rest of the world doesn't know who you really are, and the people you come into contact with every day will be trying to figure you out by summing you up, based on the way you present yourself to the world. They don't do this because they are mean or judgmental. They do it because it's the most natural thing in the world to do. They also do it whether or not they know they're doing it.

Similarly, the messages you are conveying through your image are very powerful whether or not you know what those messages are, and whether or not they are intentional. Your clothing, hairstyle, and grooming can transform the way others see you, as well as the way you feel about yourself. When you can look in the mirror and love the person you see, you will be beaming with confidence.

So if I were to ask you what your image says about you, what would you say? What adjectives do you think others would use to describe you? Is there an inconsistency between what you want people to think about you and the message they are getting?

What do your image, body language, and tone say about your capabilities, self-confidence, and worth?

Some people reject the idea of investing time or money into improving their appearance because they feel that it is self-centered to be focused on themselves in such a way. Others may be convinced that their image is merely a superficial detail that they do not need to be bothered with, as long as they have confidence in their intelligence and abilities — they feel that no one cares about such things. And still others have a tremendous fear of looking foolish. They may see any kind of change as threatening, or perhaps change just makes them feel uncomfortable or conspicuous.

The hard truth is that there are very few places in this world where appearance does not matter — and even in those places, a moderate amount of time spent on looking your best can help.

Contrary to what most of us have been taught, appearance does matter.

Some people resist this concept because it's challenging to learn about something that you were always convinced had no real intrinsic value. But by choosing to analyze and take charge of your image, you are not being contrived or insincere. You are just using important knowledge as a tool to ensure that you are sending the world the right message about who you are, what is important to you, and what you wish to achieve.

Now to the specifics of how you look online. Don't like the way you look on camera? Well you are not alone — most people don't. Once you have followed the guidelines in this book, however, you may change your mind. My goal is to not only help you look more polished and professional for those seeing you in online meetings or presentations, but for you to like, and feel more confident about how you look on camera.

Some people are comfortable with how they look on camera; others are definitely not. Which of the following describes you?

1. **You are okay with how you look in the mirror, but you do not like seeing yourself in photos or video.** This is a common issue, and there are good reasons for it. It could be that you are too close to the camera, which has a tendency to slightly distort your facial features. You may also be used to seeing a mirror image of yourself, which is not what you are seeing on the screen. Remember: what you see in the mirror is not how others see you.

   My solution to this is to bring your personal best (lighting, framing, clothing, hairstyle, glasses, makeup, etc.) to the online platform, and LET IT GO... really, let it go! This will allow you to show up looking confident in your online interactions. Video screens take the dark areas of our faces, such as 5 o'clock shadows on men's faces, or the under-eye circles that almost everyone has, and make them look darker. Remember, there is a reason that stylists and makeup artists are always available to people going on TV.

2. **Deep down, you do not like how you look anytime at all.** This is a deep-seated issue that really should be addressed, but it is outside the scope of this book. However, by using the advice in this book, you can take some actions that will help you feel more confident, and help you recreate the person you want to be no matter how you feel about how you look.

Every industry and office has its own culture and appropriate dress code, even if it is unspoken. Working from home has many people wondering if they really need to dress in professional attire when working from home. Do not dress just for comfort. You should dress for online meetings looking like the expert that you are. You want to convey the same professionalism you would if you were at your office making a professional call; you don't want to look as if you are showing up for this meeting as an afterthought. It is so tempting to put on leisure wear and just be comfortable when you're in your own home. But please don't fall prey to laziness and a lack of self-awareness when it comes to maintaining your professional credibility.

Makeup

Women often ask me whether they have to wear makeup to be credible. The short answer is, of course not. But as we age, most of us get dark circles under our eyes, or an uneven skin color; our lips and eye color fades, and we all start to look a little washed out. Video cameras tend to highlight the imperfections that we already don't like when we see them in the mirror. A two-minute makeup application can quickly and easily correct all of that.

Do You Look Shiny?

Your skin may not look shiny when you look in the mirror, but once you get in front of all the light that it takes to look good in virtual meetings, you will see a lot of skin reflection. That needs to be toned down with some foundation powder or blotting powder.

Why? Shiny skin can really sabotage your credibility. When people are lying or nervous, one of the telltale signs is sweating. So if you want to look calm, cool, collected — and honest! — you need to get rid of the shine. Here's how:

Before   *After*

For Women

For online meetings, think about evening your skin tone with powder, foundation, or concealer. Adding some blush and lip color can make a huge difference. Due to the reflections from so much direct lighting, avoid shimmery, iridescent, or pearlized makeup products that reflect light, which will draw attention to your makeup.

Eye makeup is optional, but I personally don't go online without it. I use contour in the eye crease to open and define the eye in a soft matte light brown shade, a dark brown liner, and mascara. Some people may want to subtly define their brows.

And don't forget the most important makeup tip: eliminate the shine with powder.

For Men

Men have always worn makeup for TV appearances. Getting rid of the shine is paramount for men too. Powder application is highly recommended to eliminate shine. Roger Riggle's Blot powder is easy to order online, and is my favorite powder for both men and women. It also works for all skin tones. This product is strictly for reducing shine and does not "even" your skin tone. If you need to cover dark circles or blemishes as well, take advantage of corrective products that correct dark circles or blemishes. Roger Riggle products can also help you with any makeup issues you may have for on-camera meetings. Blotting powder can be purchased at rogerriggle.com. (When asked if you want a "pan" or a "compact," choose compact.)

Best Colors for Presenting On-Camera

What should you wear for online meetings and presentations?

Every organization has its own culture for dress. Take cues from the top, and if in doubt, dress up, not down.

For Men

The camera prefers solid color shirts and jackets versus prints. Video cameras sometimes have a hard time reading the details and patterns of checks and plaids, so choose a solid color shirt if possible. Avoid wearing either very light (especially white) shirts, or very dark ones. Any shade of blue always works. Collared shirts are also available in other colors, including pink, coral, or lavender; avoid yellow, green, beige, and tan. If you are wearing a suit or sports jacket, stay away from earth tones or black, and go for navy or mid-tone gray.

Five ways to look more polished and confident on camera.

For Women

When you are wearing a jacket (blazer), blouse or dress, do not choose black or white. Why? Anything the camera sees that is very dark or very light greatly affects the exposure that the camera will adjust to, which can end up having too much contrast. Mid-tone colors look great on camera. Mid-tones and jewel tones are ideal.

What are mid-tones? Basically, anything that is not considered "light," "pastel," or "dark."

Here some examples of mid-tone colors:

These colors complement skin tones and separate you from the background; they are also more memorable than dark or pastel colors. Additionally, these shades "play well" with lighting, unlike light colors (which reflect the light), or dark colors (which absorb the light).

Remember to choose colors that *do not* blend into your background!

You want "separation" from the background to draw attention to you. And, if you are using a green screen to get the best quality in you virtual background, do not wear any shade of green!

Avoid prints, unless the blouse is being worn underneath a jacket. A cream or white shell is fine under a jacket for women, but you should avoid white and pastel blouses if you are wearing them without a jacket.

You should also avoid earth tones such as olive green, rust, camel, tan, beige, or brown. These colors do not test well for camera appearance or credibility, nor do they usually look good next to most skin tones.

Shiny fabrics should be avoided because they reflect light. Anything stretchy must fit perfectly, or it tends to look too casual. Be very discerning with scoop or V-neck tops — they tend to look lower when on camera. If in doubt, choose something else. The rules of dressing for an informal or creative environment are more difficult to decipher, but that doesn't mean that they don't exist.

Even in business settings, there will sometimes be those who stretch the rules of what is appropriate. Instead of copying what they are wearing, think about what would work best for you. If you have always worn jackets to the office in the past, you can still wear a jacket (even though it may feel odd since you may be sitting in your living room) or choose a dress or blouse that conveys professionalism as well.

For women, choosing the right clothing made out of the right fabric can get complicated — particularly in winter, when turtlenecks and sweaters are an easy choice. Avoid wearing sweater fabrics on camera. They tend to make you look frumpy. Choose a blouse, dress, or jacket made of a less casual fabric instead, to give your outline more structure.

Tilt the sides of your glasses up about one and a half inches above your ear to avoid reflections.

Accessories

Accessories should be used sparingly, and be minimal in size. Avoid anything reflective and shiny, as well as sparkles, dangling earrings, "statement" jewelry, and things that take the attention away from your face (such as anything too shiny or large). Save your statement pieces and "fun" clothing for socializing, not for work.

Fixing Glare from Glasses

Glasses are challenging for anyone on camera. With all the lighting necessary for looking great on camera, if you wear glasses you will surely have reflections on the glass that keep people from seeing your eyes. Don't worry! You can use a simple technique used by TV stars and journalists: Just tilt the sides of your glasses up about one and a half inches above your ear. This always does the trick! It feels odd, but it looks great on camera! And even with progressives this will not alter your vision.

Remember, what you wear each day broadcasts to the world **so much** information about who you are.

Intentional dressing means deliberately creating an image for yourself that will send the right message. And dressing for credibility means finding the right colors, fit, and style for you and your world. So, when preparing for meetings or presentations, ask yourself these questions before you get dressed:

Who will be there?
What do I wish to achieve?
What impression do I want to leave?

Getting dressed with intention each day is not an obligation, and it's not about being attractive; it's an opportunity to tell the world, with professionalism and presence, that you value yourself, you are capable, and you are an asset to your organization.

CHAPTER NINE

Time Management: Maximizing Your Productivity When Working From Home

Time management is an essential skill to develop whether you are working from the office or remotely. By utilizing proven techniques for efficient management of your time, you can reduce stress and increase your productivity.

Time management is not just asking, "What is the best use of my time?" It is a tool that can help you become more empowered in the workplace.

Here are a few essential tips for working from home:

1. **Set up a dedicated workspace.**
   Working from home is challenging. Online meetings require a good internet connection, so you want to be out of the way of other people, but near your router. Try to pick a quiet area that has no people coming and going or holding conversations. Find a comfortable but supportive chair and, if necessary put a pillow behind you so you can sit up straight in meetings.

2. **Prioritize your to-do list.**
   What? You don't have a to-do list? List making may not be for everyone, but for most people it can help you stay focused, reduce procrastination, and avoid forgetting to do important things.

Here are some ideas:

- You may want to try keeping two weekly lists: one for home, and one for work. Sometimes, when working from home we feel an overlap on what is demanding our time. (Should I start the dishwasher? Oh, yikes, I need to do some laundry. Maybe I should make my grocery list... And so on.) Pretend you are at the office, and stick with the task of focusing on work. By prioritizing your list, you will not be caught stressing out about not completing something urgent.

3. **Stop multitasking.** Performing two or more tasks at once may make you feel like a superhero, but the research shows that it can reduce productivity up to 40 percent. According to the *Harvard Business Review,* multitaskers do less and miss information.

You may be getting email alerts and text messages on your phone from friends who don't realize you are busy at work. You may welcome the interruption at times, but consider putting your phone on airplane mode and check in when you have completed your tasks.

4. **Don't surf the web or peek at social media.** It's right there calling you...the compelling world of surfing the web or scrolling through social media. Don't start. It's like a potato chip — it's hard to have just one.

5. **Schedule your breaks and lunchtime, and stick to the schedule.** Taking a break from screen time and occasionally tedious meetings can reduce stress and energize your brain. Your break should include getting up and walking away from your computer. You need time away from your screen. A break should not be used to return emails or phone calls.

6. **Do not send personal emails or tend to personal business unless it's during your break or lunchtime.** You can do all of those items on your to-do list; you just have to do them at the right time.

7. **Set work/life boundaries so you do not feel like you are living at work.** Don't answer work calls or emails after hours unless it is urgent. This can be challenging. Changing from work clothes to casual clothing when your work hours are over helps; getting away from your computer and being present with something not work-related after hours is highly recommended.

8. **Set clear expectations of your work hours, both for yourself and for colleagues or clients.**

9. **Don't schedule events on your calendar without thinking about how you want to structure your day.** Take your own personal biorhythms, energy, and focus into consideration when planning what you will do when.

10. **To get into the work mode, put on your work clothes!**

CHAPTER TEN

Tips for Speakers, Presenters, and Meeting Attendees

When you are addressing your colleagues or clients in a webinar or conference, *you* get to choose how *you* will be perceived by them. Good content that is well-delivered is important, but paying close attention to the way you look on your screen by carefully arranging the framing, lighting, camera, and angles will help keep people engaged in what you are saying.

Whether you want to inspire, educate, get people to take action, or get them to support your ideas, the tips below can help ensure that your presentation will receive the attention it deserves:

1. Engaging your viewers in virtual presentations is much different than in-person presentations. It's critical to get your framing right so that your body language can add dynamic energy to your presentation. Presenters should consider standing instead of sitting, which provides the advantage of choosing a wider frame for yourself than you would have just sitting in front of a computer. But remember, if you stand, your computer also has to be raised to a higher level. **The camera always has to be at eye level.**

   If you are sitting you should be framed from the lower chest up, with your head barely below the top of the screen. When you are standing, you should be framed from the *waist* up so that your hands can gesture and be seen instead of popping up wildly into the frame. In both cases, your head should be at the top of the screen. (See Chapter 2 for more detail about how to achieve optimal framing.)

2. Use an external microphone. (See Chapter 4 for how to choose one.)

3. Many people have a habit of talking too quickly: if you are a fast talker, train yourself to consciously slow down. This is more important in online presentations than it is for in-person interactions.

4. Do not have your inflection go up at the end of a sentence as if it were a question. Most people do not know they are doing this but it can sabotage your credibility. Record yourself presenting, and see if your statements sound like questions. You can also ask a trusted colleague for their input.

5. Become aware of how frequently you are peppering your speech with *umms* and *ahhs*. One way you can do this is to record yourself talking before a presentation: this is the best way for you to know how you sound to others, and identify what you want to work on changing.

6. Present to the camera lens: ***do not*** look at your screen. You might want to tape a colorful post-it note behind your camera to remind you where to look.

7. Don't wear white or black. Mid-tone colors are preferred and do not include pastels. Pastels and white can be used under a jacket. (*See Chapter 8*.)

8. The tone of your voice can tell people whether you are happy or sad, excited and engaged, or bored. Become conscious of your voice inflection and be sure to vary it, to make your content more interesting for your listeners — and fun to listen to.

9. Smiling and using positive body language when you are speaking shows that you are confident about what you are saying.

10. If your meeting has been called to discuss a challenge, don't start your talk with a sad commentary about the state of things. Instead, welcome people to the meeting as you would in person. ("Thanks everyone, for being here.") You might want to start the meeting with a question, or make an emphatic statement like, "I am excited by the upcoming changes..."

11. Have a clear agenda. Be sure you have thought out not only what you want to achieve in this meeting, but how you are going to organize the discussion so that your goal can be achieved.

12. If someone contradicts or challenges you, saying things like "I'm glad you brought that up," or "I'm concerned about that too," or "Thank you for clarifying that..." can help keep the discussion positive and productive.

13. Do not use video as part of your presentation in your online meetings. Because of connectivity issues, videos tend to freeze, or lag visually from the audio and create a frustration experience for the viewer. If video is an important part of your presentation, send a link to the video for others to view before or after your online presentation.

"

pro·to·col

noun
Business Protocol
The accepted, or established code of
procedure or behavior in an organization.

"

Tips and Etiquette for Meeting Attendees

1. You can leave a powerful and lasting impression with your colleagues or clients by speaking up, clearly, and with warmth and enthusiasm. Remember to wait until the speaker invites interaction so you aren't interrupting the flow of the meeting.

2. When you speak be sure to look directly at the camera, not at the video screen. This will help the other viewers feel like you are looking at them.

3. Never "preen" while on camera: no fixing your hair or stroking your beard!

4. Choose a voice tone and inflection that conveys sincerity and interest.

5. Don't talk too fast, and don't mumble! Above all, keep your hands away from your face when you are speaking.

6. If you are introducing a new topic, or a topic that is tangential to the main discussion, keep it short. You might want to just briefly mention the issue, and suggest that it can be followed up off-line with the relevant party or parties when you are not in a group session.

7. Sign into the meeting looking attentive: sitting up straight, and be sure you have set up a well-lit and framed video image.

8. When it is appropriate, you can smile, or nod your head with approval or agreement when others are speaking: do **not** look down, or multitask during the meeting.

9. Unless you are invited to do so by the speaker, don't eat or drink during the meeting.

10. Do not distract other participants: turn your video off if there is something you need to tend to or if you need to get up.

CHAPTER ELEVEN

Leadership: Meeting the Challenges of Online Meetings

t's critical for organizations to acknowledge the challenges of our teams that are working from home or interacting with clients or boards only through an online platform. There is a unique kind of stress that comes from struggling with technology issues, seeing yourself on camera, and staring at a screen all day instead of interacting with people in person.

It's called brain fatigue, and we have all experienced it in online meetings. It sets in when we get tired — and not very productive — as a result of too much screen time. Most people can handle excessive screen time occasionally, but when it's habitual, eventually it takes its toll, psychologically and physically, on everyone.

Not interacting with co-workers has a huge impact on staying motivated. In addition, there is the issue of staying organized, managing your time, and remembering to take breaks.

Are any of these statements true for you or members of your team?

- I spend too much time just looking at a screen.
- I have too many meetings in a day.
- My meetings last too long.
- I am sitting all day, and I don't have enough time to get up and move around.
- I am frustrated by the technological issues of working at home (slow internet speed, lighting issues, audio problems, the way I look).

Executives and managers need to be aware of these tell-tale signs of burnout among their employees:

- Excessive multitasking or fidgeting
- Lack of eye contact
- Body language that may be screaming, "I'm worn out!" (This includes signs like video cameras being turned off, head rubbing, or employees looking disheveled),

When employees physically go to a workplace all day, there is so much more opportunity to move around and have spontaneous interactions with people than in a situation where most people are working from home. The challenge then is keeping people motivated, engaged, and inspired to do their best work, even from home.

It's no surprise that most people are not inspired by looking at a computer screen all day long. That's why keeping your video on during meetings is essential to engaging and inspiring your team. Their body language may tell you more than their words.

In addition to the challenges presented by burnout, you may not have a consensus as to what the protocol or proper etiquette is for online meetings at your organization.

How can people know how to interact professionally if there are no guidelines or expectations for them to follow?

I suggest creating an Online Meeting Protocol for your organization. I have created a free blueprint that you can use, or you can edit the template to create your own. Go to www.kimfoley.com to download the blueprint.

During consultations, I repeatedly get these questions relating to online protocol:

- Do I always need my camera on?
- Is it okay to eat on camera?
- What should I do if I need to briefly leave the room?
- What should I be wearing for various types of meetings?
- How do I minimize distractions and procrastination?

We all know that optics matter. But for some people, dressing appropriately might be challenging when working from home. Wrangling toddlers and feeding children while working is quite the feat! In these circumstances, some flexibility of the usual rules may be in order: everyone should not have to be in corporate dress for every meeting. However, executives may want to consider clarifying proper dress guidelines for their team leaders, management, those giving presentations, and especially those who are meeting with board members or interacting with clients.

Keep in mind that the top two reasons that people disengage and turn off their video is because either they do not like how they look on camera, or they are embarrassed about their surroundings and want privacy.

The bottom line is that most people are struggling to get it right, and no one wants to look foolish. Providing employees with guidelines can be helpful in this regard.

You might want to consider hiring a professional to help your team with working from home issues, such as setting up a workspace for productivity and comfort, or creating better visuals through basic techniques of lighting, framing, camera angles, background, and audio issues, as well as suggestions on which clothing works best for on-screen meetings.

If you want to increase your team's productivity and morale, here are a few ideas that some of my clients are implementing in their organizations to minimize burnout and fatigue:

- Whenever possible, determine the maximum length of the meeting in advance, and keep it as short as possible. You don't have to use all of the allotted time if the business of the meeting is completed earlier. No one is going to mind early dismissal!

- Ask your employees to create space in their calendars (30 minutes twice a day, in addition to a lunch break) for getting up and moving around, eating a snack, or taking a brief walk. Such breaks from screen time are essential, both for employees' health and for maintaining optimal productivity.

- If that doesn't work for your organization, consider implementing a 15-minute break between meetings.

- Remember: every meeting does not have to be a video meeting. Could a conference call suffice?

- Don't schedule an online meeting when an email will do just as well.

If you want to help your team to increase their professionalism in virtual meetings or presentations visit www.kimfoley.com where you can learn more about live, virtual training available for individuals, groups, and conferences.

Glossary

Background What viewers see in the background behind you.

Bandwidth Bandwidth refers to the maximum capacity of your internet connection measured in megabits (Mbps).

Bluetooth The short-range wireless interconnection of mobile phones, computers, and other electronic devices.

Bluetooth microphone Wireless, short-range audio data transferred between devices

Bluetooth headset Headphones that are not hard-wired, but connect wirelessly to help you hear others better online.

Earphones A small piece of equipment that is worn inside or over the ear to listen to a recording or online presentation.

Earbuds Small earphones, worn inside the outer ear.

External microphone A microphone that is not built into your computer, headset, or camera.

Foreground Whatever is closest to the camera (generally, you).

Framing Placement of the subject in relation to other objects. Good framing can make an image more aesthetically pleasing, and hold the viewer's attention.

Hardwire To connect electronic components or devices by electrical wires or cables.

Hard-wired, or external microphones Microphones that are connected via cable to your computer or webcam.

Lavalier A small microphone intended to clip onto clothing. Lavaliere microphones can be either wireless (Bluetooth), or hard-wired.

Online platform Has been used to describe a range of services available on the internet, including marketplaces, search engines, social media, creative content outlets, app stores, communications services, and payment systems.

Router/Modem Interface from your internet service provider (Verizon, Comcast, etc.) That creates your local network and broadcasts your WiFi signal.

Reboot or restart Turn computer completely off, and then restart it.

Speed Internet speed is often mistaken for bandwidth. Speed is how quickly the information is received or downloaded, and is calculated in Mbps.

Synced Programs or software on your digital device that can recognize each other, and are coordinated.

Sources Consulted

Ambady, N., Rosenthal, R. 1992. "Thin slices of expressive behavior as predictors of interpersonal consequences: A meta-analysis." *Psychological Bulletin* 111 (2): 256.

Bourel, F., Chibelushi, C., Low, A. 2002. "Robust facial expression recognition using a state-based model of spatially-localised facial dynamics." In: IEEE Automatic Face and Gesture Recognition.

Cook, S., Goldin-Meadow, S. 2006. "The role of gesture in learning: Do children use their hands to change their minds?" *Journal of Cognition and Development* 7 (2): 211–232.

De Gelder, B. 2006. "Towards the neurobiology of emotional body language." *Nature Reviews Neuroscience* 7 (3): 242–249.

De Gelder, B. 2009. "Why bodies? Twelve reasons for including bodily expressions in affective neuroscience." *Phil. Trans. of the Royal Society B* 364 (1535): 3475.

Ekenel, H., Stiefelhagen, R. 2006. "Block selection in the local appearance-based face recognition scheme." In: Computer Vision and Pattern Recognition Workshop. pp. 43. IEEE.

Ekman, P., Friesen, W. 1969. "The repertoire of nonverbal behavior: Categories, origins, usage, and coding." *Semiotica* 1(1): 49–98.

Goldin-Meadow, S. 2005. *Hearing Gesture: How Our Hands Help Us Think.* Belknap Press.

Goldin-Meadow, S., Wagner, S. 2005. "How our hands help us learn." *Trends in Cognitive Sciences* 9(5): 234–241.

Gunes, H., Piccardi, M. 2006. "A bimodal face and body gesture database for automatic analysis of human nonverbal affective behavior." In: *International Conference on Pattern Recognition.* Vol. 1, pp. 1148–1153. IEEE.

el Kaliouby, R., Robinson, P. 2005. "Real-time vision for human computer interaction," In: *Real-Time Inference of Complex Mental States from Facial Expressions and Head Gestures,* pp. 181–200. Springer-Verlag.

Lucey, P., Cohn, J., Kanade, T., Saragih, J., Ambadar, Z., Matthews, I. 2010. "The extended Cohn-Kanade dataset (CK+): A complete dataset for action unit and emotion-specified expression." In: Computer Vision and Pattern Recognition Workshop. pp. 94–101. IEEE.

About The Author

Kim Foley

Founder, Smartphone Video Production Academy, award-winning video producer, corporate trainer, television stylist, author

Training and Consultations

Virtual Meetings With Impact and Presence

Research shows that *image matters*. How you are perceived is critical for building credibility, especially in virtual meetings. We will uncover the pitfalls online that are not present during traditional in-person meetings. Learn how to interact online — so you enhance, rather than detract from, your underlying business objectives.This session will help you troubleshoot technical challenges in addition to addressing framing, best audio options, body language, and clothing recommendations. This training is available for one-on one sessions or for groups.

Media Training and Image Consulting For Online or Video Presentations

Kim Foley provides Media Training for those who do recorded video, live or online presentations or television appearances. This one-on-one, confidential training helps clients learn how to maximize their presentation skills, manage fear, avoid body language pitfalls and enhance their credibility. Learn the nuance of voice inflection and pacing and how to read a teleprompter. Individualized wardrobe, hairstyling and makeup consultation are included. This training is available in-person or online.

Speaker

As a speaker on innovation and digital media, she is a dynamic workshop leader for conferences. Topics Include:

- Virtual Meetings With Power and Presence
- 5 Ways To Sabotage or Enhance You Credibility
- How You Look, What You Say And How You Say It

Smartphone Video Production And Editing

Kim Foley is an award-winning video producer, and the founder of Smartphone Video Production Academy. Her passion is helping businesses join the video revolution. Ms. Foley has developed innovative, training programs that teaches organizations how to use the advances in smartphone technology to create and edit professional quality video all on a smartphone or tablet. Her clients include ExxonMobil, The Jewish Federation, Nestle, as well as government agencies and nonprofits.

Television Makeup and Wardrobe Styling

When public figures need to look their best, they turn to Kim Foley. For more than 25 years, as a professional wardrobe and makeup stylist for film and television, Ms. Foley has worked with hundreds of high-profile clients, including Presidents Barack Obama, George Bush and Bill Clinton, Jay Leno, Stephen Colbert, Brian Williams, and the list goes on. She has worked for *Meet the Press* and *60 Minutes* as well as productions for ABC, NBC, CBS, HBO, MTV, BBC, Lifetime, The Discovery Channel, and feature films. She has worked on hundreds of commercials, teleconferences, press conferences, and government films for agencies such as FBI, CIA, IRS, NIH and FDA.

Author, Virtual Meetings With Power and Presence 2020
Author, The Credibility Factor: The Smart Woman's Guide To A More Powerful Presence 2006

kimfoley.com

Virtual Training Sessions

Virtual Meetings with Impact and Presence
Live, Online One-On-One Training
Inquire about group sessions or in-house webinars.

How you look, what you say and how you say it screams your value to the world. Your credibility is one of your most valuable assets. This online presentation training is a confidence-building experience that will provide your executives or your team with the essential skills and techniques they need to look professional and to comfortably and effectively participate in online meetings and presentations or recorded video presentations and webinars. This training is customized to meet the unique challenges and needs of each individual and organization.

Includes:

1. **On-Camera Presentation Skills for Online Meetings**
   - Technology and device preparation for maximizing internet connection
   - How to get the best audio
   - Learn how to properly frame yourself on the screen
   - How to get the best framing and angles
   - Learn how to create the best lighting
   - Avoid body language blunders
   - Learn the best techniques for sitting or standing
   - Learn where you should be looking
   - Virtual meeting best practices (online etiquette)
   - Learn techniques to deal with nervousness

2. **Individual Wardrobe and Makeup Consultation**
   (Not included in group training)
   - Individualized advice on hairstyle, grooming and makeup
   - Assessment of current clothing options
   - Advice on accessories and glasses
   - Suggestions for clothing styles and color for online video meetings and presentations

By recognizing and understanding the symbols of authority, the language of clothing and the powerful nuances involved in nonverbal communications, participants will gain enhanced confidence and increase their credibility in online meetings and presentations. All sessions are confidential.

Produce and Edit Professional Quality Smartphone Video
Live, One-On-One Online Training

Now you can learn how to produce and edit professional-quality videos for your business with a quick turnaround and a tight budget. This cutting-edge training will teach even the most technologically challenged how to create professional quality videos with a smartphone. This is a hands-on, 2-hour, interactive, online training.

Learn to:
- Focus and white-balance the camera
- Create professional lighting
- Frame your subject to maximize credibility
- Create professional-quality audio
- Master online presentation skills
- Pros and cons of various equipment options
- Teleprompter basics and options
- Upload your video to social media, 3rd party platforms or in-house servers

iPhone Video Editing
One-Hour Training

Want a fast turn-around for your videos?

In this training you will learn how to professionally edit your video all on your mobile phone or iPad.

Learn to:
- Cut footage
- Change the camera's focal length
- Adjust volume
- Add titles, Lower thirds
- Create smooth transitions
- Create end slide
- Add music, voiceover, photos
- Change speed
- How to save and upload to various platforms
- And much more

On-Camera Media Training
Two-Hour Training

Managing the way you are perceived on camera is critical in building credibility. Whether you are doing live presentations or pre-taping on-camera, your on-camera persona is one of your most valuable assets.

On-camera Media Training is a confidence-building experience that will provide you with the essential skills and techniques you need to comfortably and effectively speak on camera and engage on video for presentations or appearances.

This training is customized to meet the unique challenges and needs of each individual and includes:

- On-camera practice and feedback (with and without teleprompter)
- Learning the techniques of reading a teleprompter
- Learning the best way to open and close your video
- How to use voice inflection for pauses
- Helpful techniques for dealing with nervousness or fear
- Cues that will help you be seen as the expert
- How to avoid body language blunders
- Getting comfortable with lighting and microphones
- Learning the best techniques for sitting or standing
- Learning where you should be looking

Notes

Made in the USA
Coppell, TX
28 October 2020

40345649R00055